DOLLY PARTON

DOLLY PARTON

JUDITH MAHONEY PASTERNAK

MetroBooks

An Imprint of Friedman/Fairfax Publishers

© 1998 by Michael Friedman Publishing Group, Inc.

Library of Congress Cataloging-in-Publication data available upon request.

ISBN 1-56799-557-8

Line Editor: Traci Cothran
Editors: Francine Hornberger and Reka Simonsen
Designers: Andrea Karman and Maria Mann
Photography Editor: Amy Talluto

Color separations by Bright Arts Graphics (s) Pte Ltd
Printed in Singapore by KHL Printing Co. Pte Ltd

10 9 8 7 6 5 4 3 2 1

For bulk purchases and special sales, please contact:
Friedman/Fairfax Publishers
Attention: Sales Department
15 West 26th Street
New York, NY 10010
212/685-6610 FAX 212/685-1307

Visit our website:
http://www.metrobooks.com

Dedication

This is for all the parents—Dolly's, mine, and those whose names are yet unknown—who taught their girl-children that it really was all right for them to know what they wanted.

Acknowledgements

I thank the staff of the Country Music Foundation—otherwise known as country researcher's heaven—who sat me down in front of all the boxes labeled "Dolly" on a rainy day in Nashville and let me browse in them. I thank my editor, Francine Hornberger, for her uncanny ability to zero in on every paragraph, sentence, or word I wasn't sure of, and to help me find a way to make it right. And, as always, I thank my dear friend and co-conspirator Chris Seymour, for refusing to let me turn in a manuscript he hasn't read.

TABLE OF CONTENTS

Introduction

"**I**t costs a lot to make a person look this cheap," says Dolly Parton.

The money is well spent. The tiny beauty with the sweet voice has parlayed a big bust, bigger wigs, her own theme park, and her own wry sense of humor into a show-biz fortune: Dolly is one of the wealthiest women in the business.

She's also one of the most respected—and one of the most beloved. Everybody loves Parton, from hard-bitten rock writers like *Rolling Stone's* Chet Flippo to radical feminists like *Ms.* founder Gloria Steinem. Although the *People*-reading public has followed her every move for almost thirty years and her records have crossed over from country music to pop again and again, country fans still see her as one of their own, among the last of the rags-to-riches country stars. And among professional musicians of every stripe, she's one of the nation's best and most prolific songwriters.

Much of her popularity is due to her talents—including her gift for projecting a persona of such immense appeal. Dolly's uncanny mix of candor and coyness has intrigued audiences and critics alike from the start of her career. Frank about her age, for instance, she remains charmingly vague about dates and details; she was somewhere between twelve and fourteen when she made her first

Previous Photo: **Dolly is almost as famous for her sex appeal as she is for her beautiful voice.**
Right: **Dolly and Kenny Rogers performing their 1983 megahit, "Islands in the Stream."**

Dolly Parton
12

record and she has hinted that she may have been even younger when she first experimented with sex. When interviewers ask, "Exactly when was that?" Dolly sweetly but efficiently changes the subject. And although she speaks freely of a close relationship with God, she has never specified what religious denomination she was born into or follows.

One thing she is never vague about, however, is where she comes from. On the long road from poverty to success she has stayed close to her roots. Her theme park, Dollywood, is only a few miles from the mountainside where she was born, in Sevier County, Tennessee, in 1946....

Opposite: **Dolly's lush figure—and her sense of humor about it—helped create the image that set her apart from other country singers...** *Right:* **...and earned her a star on Hollywood Boulevard's Walk of Fame.**

CHAPTER ONE

Dirt Poor in Sevier County

$\mathcal{L}$ike many of the chapters of Dolly's life story, the account of her birth verges on an American archetype. It begins with a doctor on horseback, fighting his way through a fierce mountain snowstorm to reach the one-room cabin where twenty-two-year-old Avie Lee Owens Parton lay in labor with her fourth child. The cabin had no street address; Dr. Thomas got there by turning onto a rough track from the Pittman Center Road that runs up Andy Manier Mountain along the banks of the Little Pigeon River, not far from Gatlinburg, in the Great Smoky Mountains of Tennessee.

It was January 19, 1946, and the family he was going to help was straight out of mountain myth. In the middle of the twentieth century, Robert Lee Parton and his wife and children were living very much as his Scotch-Irish ancestors had a century before. Robert Lee was a sharecropper, a tobacco farmer eking out a living. Money was in such short supply that he paid Dr. Thomas for the delivery of Dolly Rebecca with a sack of cornmeal.

Cash-poor as they were, the mountain folk were nevertheless hardy. Of Robert and Avie Lee's twelve children, all but one survived, and these grew up knowing all four of their grandparents: Robert Lee's father and mother, William Walter Parton (always called Walter) and Bessie Rayfield Parton, and Avie Lee's part-

Previous Photo: **Dolly's Grandpa Jake Owens (left), the "Old Time Preacher Man," and Grandma Rena Owens (second from left), with Dolly's mother, Avie Lee Parton, and her children. Fourteen-year-old Dolly is at top right.** *Right:* **Dolly at three and a half among the mountain grasses and flowers.**

Cherokee, part Scotch-Irish parents, Jake Owens and Rena Kansas Valentine Owens. The frailest of the grandparents, Grandma Bessie Parton, was bedridden (with what may have been an inner-ear ailment) for as long as any of her grandchildren remembered, but even so, she lived to be seventy-seven.

The sense of stern Southern religion ran more strongly in the Owens family than among the Partons, but one thing both families approved of was secular music. "Rev." Jake Owens, a schoolteacher and lay preacher, who reputedly never took a drink or smoked a cigarette in his life, sang as a matter of course, often writing his own songs. A skilled country fiddler as well as a man of God, Rev. Jake penned "Singing His Praise," which early country superstar Kitty Wells recorded.

Robert (second row, center) and Avie Lee Parton (second row, right) with their eight eldest children: Willadeene (second row, left) and (front row, left to right) David, Cassie, Stella, Dolly (seven years old), baby Randy, Bobby, and Denver. Avie Lee was not yet thirty when this photograph was taken.

Most of his children followed suit. Avie Lee, who played guitar and sang to her children all their lives, eventually cut a couple of records as Smoky Mountain Mama. Four of his other children—Dolly's uncles Bill, Louis, and Henry, and her aunt Dorothy Jo Hope—were songwriters. Both Avie Lee's spiritual and musical inheritance would descend in force to her children.

As Dolly describes it, "My momma's people and my daddy's people grew up as good friends, that's how they met. There's a lot of marriages between the Partons and the Owenses." Robert and Avie Lee married in 1939, when he was seventeen and she was fifteen; she was pregnant within months of the marriage.

But there were problems, at least at the beginning of the marriage. Robert continued to roam the hills and small towns at night with his bachelor friends, leaving Avie Lee alone in their mountainside cabin. Revealing a streak of assertiveness that would become another legacy to her daughters, Avie Lee left him and went home to her parents. Only after the birth of her first child, Dolly's older sister Willadeene, did Avie Lee let Robert persuade her to come back to him.

They reconciled with a vengeance. All twelve of their children were born before Avie Lee's thirty-fifth birthday. After Willadeene came David, Denver, Dolly, Bobby, Stella, Cassie, Larry (who lived only nine hours), Randy, the twins Floyd and Freida, and Rachel. "Momma had kids all the time," Dolly recalls a little sadly. "She had one on her and one in her. She was always pregnant, and the time she wasn't pregnant, she was just really rundown sick." The older children helped care for the younger ones. Avie Lee made a ritual of "giving" each new baby, in turn, to an older sibling; at six, Willadeene became a second mother to the infant Dolly.

When Dolly was six or so, she was supposed to be "given" a baby of her own, but instead the family suffered a painful loss. As Dolly tells it, "Momma took spinal meningitis....The doctor said there was no way she could live....He told Daddy and my Grandma she wouldn't live through the night. So they had church that night and they prayed all night." (They also kept Avie Lee packed in ice throughout the anxious vigil to bring down her fever.) "And the next mornin', when the doctor came in, Momma...said, 'I've been healed.' "

But Avie Lee was pregnant at the time and the fever fatally injured the baby she was carrying. Shortly afterward she gave birth to Larry, who died nine hours later. The baby's death left Dolly more bereft than it did her siblings because Larry was supposed to be "hers." On and off over the next several years, she would feel his presence near her.

The majority of the Parton children would become musicians. Willadeene, Stella, Cassie, Rachel, Randy, and Floyd would all write songs, and several of them would make records. None of them, however, would be as prolific as the fourth child, little Dolly Rebecca, who made up songs—and sang them—as naturally as she breathed. Growing up, she often cajoled her siblings into listening to her.

Later on, Dolly would say that music, God, and sex were the forces that ruled her. If it was her Owens inheritance that provided the first two, it was the farm that gave her her earthy appreciation of the latter; her sex education came not from the birds and bees, but from pigs and chickens—and, she has hinted, from some of her older cousins. (If there were a lot of Parton siblings, there were even more cousins. Dolly describes some of them as "double cousins"—cousins on both the Parton and the Owens sides of the family.)

In the woods and fields, Dolly found a synthesis of all three forces in the spiritualized sensuality of the wild winged creatures, but most especially the butterfly. Throughout her childhood and into maturity, the butterfly seemed to be

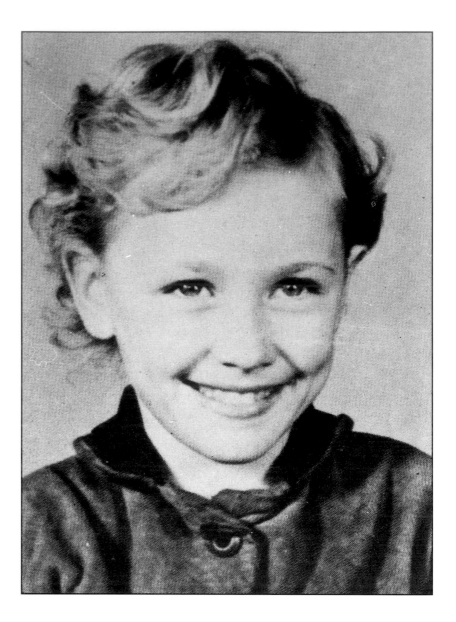

Early in her childhood, an earthy zest for life combined with spiritual striving to shape the person Dolly would become.

Robert and Avie Lee Parton in the early 1990s.

her kindred spirit; eventually, it became both her career logo and a nickname within the family. "They were always like little spiritual beings to me," she says. "Butterflies were able to fly over the mountains and see what was there, yet they could still be content where they were."

Willadeene says that the family lived a "hard, simple life" on the farm, but both she and Dolly describe it as happy—at least for the children. Everyone worked, with Robert and Avie Lee carrying the brunt of the labor and whatever worries there were about money. Early on, Robert had had another source of income: "My daddy used to make moonshine when he and Momma were first married," Dolly says, but he "got out of it because Momma didn't like it." If he remained a little fonder of the local product than Avie Lee would have preferred, he was well within the norm for the men in the community. If Avie Lee was care- and childbirth-worn, she was nevertheless always there for her children. Discipline was stern but fair. Dolly remembers if the children lied, or disappeared, or hurt each other, Robert "whipped us," yet neither Willadeene nor Dolly has expressed any doubt that their parents deeply loved all of their children.

The Country
Dolly Grew Up With

Dolly was in the right place at the right time to become a queen of country music. She and "country"—the category, not the music—were actually born in the same year, and it was during her childhood that women began to carve out room for themselves among country's pantheon of stars.

Rural and Southern America had been listening to commercial "barn dance" and "hillbilly" music for more than two decades. It was in the 1920s that the infant radio and recording industries discovered and popularized the traditional music that had been played and sung at dances and parties throughout the South since colonial days. *The Grand Ole Opry* began broadcasting over WSM, Nashville, in 1925, although during its first year it was called *The WSM Barn Dance*, and Jimmy Rodgers made his first recording in 1927.

Later, World War II and the migrations it brought about helped spread the popularity of hillbilly music far beyond its Southern base. But "hillbilly" had negative connotations, and in 1946—the year Dolly was born—guitar innovator Ernest Tubb rechristened the music "country."

1950s country trailblazer

Kitty Wells

The hardships of the war had made a rough-and-tough version of country more palatable to country audiences. Rooted in a vision of life as hard work and equally hard release, "honky-tonk" took off in the early postwar years, with Hank Williams as its foremost exponent. Hank's first big hit, "Move It on Over," was released in 1947, when Dolly was a year old.

The same year, a quiet Nashville native made her debut on *The Grand Ole Opry:* Kitty Wells (born Muriel Deason), who would become country's first woman superstar.

By 1949, the music had gotten big enough so that a country song could become a mainstream popular hit—although, at that point, only if performed by a pop star. That year, big-band singer Margaret Whiting's cover of Floyd Tilman's honky-tonk hit "Slippin' Around" made #1 on the pop charts and became the first big country crossover smash.

In mainstream pop, 1930s and 1940s big-band music had made stars of dozens of women vocalists, including Whiting and also including women with country roots, like Jo Stafford and the "Nashville Nightingale," Dinah Shore. But hillbilly/country had been substantially a male preserve for its first two and a half decades, despite occasional hits by women like "Mother" Maybelle Carter and Patsy Montana, whose "I Want to Be a Cowboy's Sweetheart" had been country's first million-seller, in 1935. In the early postwar years—the years of Dolly's early childhood—that was about to change. Country women would come into their own in the 1950s, inspiring young singers across the nation—including the adolescent in Pigeon Forge—to dream of stardom.

In 1952, Hank Thompson released "The Wild Side of Life," a honky-tonk apology on behalf of wayward men that claimed they only strayed when "honky-tonk angels" lured them from the straight-and-narrow.

The message wasn't new, but this time a woman responded. The demure Kitty Wells—of all people—put the blame back where it belonged with "It Wasn't God Who Made Honky-Tonk Angels." The record propelled her to stardom, surely in part because women welcomed a song that spoke from their perspective. It was a perspective that would find a fuller expression a few short years later in the words of Loretta Lynn. In between Wells' reply to honky-tonk and Lynn's protofeminist lyrics, however, another change burst into country with rockabilly, country's answer to rock and roll.

In the early hours of 1953, the news of honky-tonk king Hank Williams' death sent shock waves across the South. Perhaps the greatest of the country singers, Hank was only twenty-nine, killed by the same rough-and-tumble lifestyle he had sung about. Yet honky-tonk itself was losing its vigor, its underlying note of struggle giving way to the ebullience that characterized "rockabilly."

Like honky-tonk, rockabilly was a largely male phenomenon at the beginning, with Elvis Presley and Jerry Lee Lewis its biggest stars. But a few high-energy women managed to force their way into its upper reaches. Young Brenda Lee—she was only three years older than Dolly—scored big with "Dynamite" in 1957, and Jean Shepherd and Wanda Jackson also had rockabilly hits.

Then came Patsy Cline, suddenly, with the most passionate woman's voice to hit country yet, wrapped in the new, lushly string-filled packaging that came to be called the Nashville sound. In 1957, Patsy's "Walkin' after Midnight" became the biggest country crossover hit to date, making it to the Top Twenty on the pop charts.

Kitty Wells, Brenda Lee, Patsy Cline—it took all of them to break the ground from which Loretta Lynn would flower. In 1960, she and husband Doolittle Lynn marketed Loretta and her first record, "Honky-Tonk Girl," to Nashville stardom. Rooted in her own experiences and those of other coal miners' daughters, Lynn's lyrics would go a long way toward adding a woman's language to the country vocabulary.

By that time young Dolly Parton had been earning money singing on radio and television for years. Yet without those predecessors she might never have imagined getting on a bus the day after her graduation from high school in June 1964, carrying shopping bags full of songs to Nashville to become a star.

Left: **Dolly (second row, center) with the rest of the Parton sisters, all grown up—and still singing.**

Opposite: **By the time she was ten, Dolly was learning to be comfortable in front of television cameras, though this snapshot caught her in an uncharacteristically self-conscious pose.**

While food and the other basic necessities of life were always provided, there was little cash for luxuries like separate beds for everyone—or indoor plumbing. The Parton children all slept tumbled together in the family's few beds, and Dolly has often recalled that when winter weather made them reluctant to leave the warmth for the cold privy outside, they would casually and unselfconsciously wet the bed.

Dolly's first experience with a flush toilet was in the home of an aunt in Knoxville. "We were so fascinated," she says, "we were afraid to use it. I just thought it was goin' to suck us right down." As for hygiene, in the summer, the family would bathe in the Little Pigeon River; in winter, "we'd wash down as far as possible, and we'd wash up as far as possible. Then, when somebody'd clear the room, we'd wash possible." She had to do that every day, "cause the kids peed on me every night." Inexplicably, Dolly insists that, despite the near-total lack of privacy, she acquired no knowledge of sex from her parents; although considering the frequency of Avie Lee's pregnancies, they "must have done it," the children apparently never heard them.

The Knoxville aunt also had the first television Dolly ever saw; the Partons had only a battery-operated radio. Dolly remembers that "every now and then if we could afford a battery... we'd listen to *The Grand Ole Opry* and *The Lone Ranger* maybe once or twice a week." But the Partons had their

own forms of entertainment. One was looking through the free catalogs that came in the mail—Avie Lee called them "wishbooks" because they "made you wish you had things you didn't have."

Each Parton child got one new pair of shoes a year; they only needed shoes from September through May, as they ran barefoot during the summer. They also received one store-bought toy every Christmas; the rest of the time they made do with rubber-band-operated wooden cars whittled by Robert and corncob dolls made by Avie Lee. Avie Lee also made many of the children's clothes. Dolly says her early hit, "Coat of Many Colors," is based on the time she went to school in a homemade patchwork coat she thought was beautiful, though her schoolmates laughed at it.

Sharecropping life in East Tennessee was in many ways less oppressive than it was elsewhere in the South. The family's landlord, Martha Williams, was not a plantation owner, but one of their own community. The Parton children called her "Aunt Marth" and mourned her deeply

when she died when Dolly was eight years old. At that point, however, the Partons were no longer Aunt Marth's tenants: Robert had bought his own farm nearby for five thousand dollars a few years before.

When Dolly explored the new farm and the land around it, she made a discovery that would have a profound influence on her: a long-abandoned chapel, covered with graffiti, littered with the debris of years—and housing a decrepit piano. Some years later, as an adolescent, she would find in the chapel a moment of truth in her lifelong spiritual quest. Meanwhile, she took two strings from the piano, which she affixed to an old mandolin she had found in the barn; it became her accompaniment when she sang to herself. Dolly learned the basics of banjo playing when she befriended a neighborhood pariah—an old man called Sawdust. (She later memorialized their friendship in her song "Applejack.")

Proud as Robert was to have become a landowner, the move had not brought any material change in the family's life. They still used a privy, washed in the river or the kitchen, and slept in a few beds. But change was in the air: the Partons were about to discover that people beyond the family liked to hear young Dolly Rebecca sing.

CHAPTER TWO

Nashville Dreams

1953 — 1964

*D*olly's mother's family, the Owenses, had already taken note of Dolly's gifts. The year she turned seven, Uncle Bill, the most ambitious of the Owens brothers, bought her a Martin acoustic guitar. Not long afterward Willadeene, Dolly, and Stella—the three oldest Parton girls—began singing at local church services. Some of the churches where the girls sang, however, were unconventional, to say the least. One Sunday, Robert had to storm the pulpit midsermon and sweep his daughters away when the preacher, a religious snake-handler, started waving what looked like venomous snakes a little too close to his girls.

Almost as soon as she learned to read and write, Dolly began writing down the songs she made up. On the whole, her schooling—and her schoolmates—never engaged her mind or heart as did the world around her and her family. There was one exception, though. When Dolly was in the third grade, she met a redhead named Judy Ogle, an athletic tomboy who was as different from Dolly as another girl could be. Yet they became fast friends; the friendship would continue through their school years and beyond. Their paths diverged for a time, but today Judy is still Dolly's best friend and her trusted assistant.

Previous Photo: **Dolly at the Grand Ole Opry in 1970.** *Right:* **Dolly at eight, already showing the mischievous grin that has appealed to audiences most of her life.**

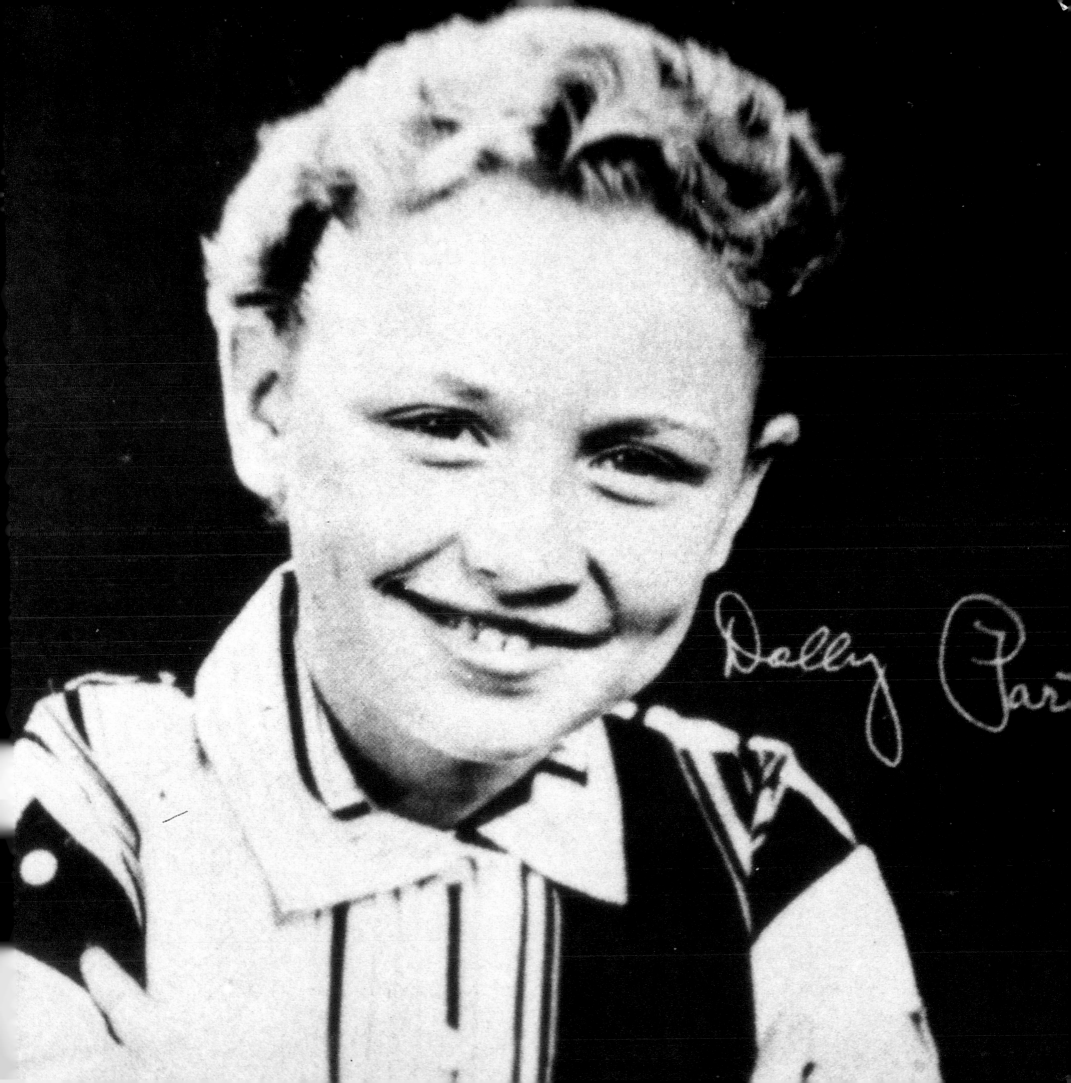

Dolly was soon taking her first steps toward a career in music. Uncle Bill used his contacts to get her an appearance on the *Cas Walker Farm and Home Hour,* a radio and television program broadcast from Knoxville, and by the time she was ten, she was singing regularly on the program. Often, she would stay over at the Knoxville home of country singers Carl and Pearl Butler, family friends whose example helped Dolly understand that you could make a living writing songs and singing them (see "Dolly's Friends Carl and Pearl Butler," on page 34-35).

The twenty dollars she brought home each time she performed was big money for the Partons. "I sang on TV before my family ever owned one," Dolly says. This income eventually provided the Partons with their first set, but it proved to be such a magnet for the television-starved population of Sevier County that Robert finally threw it away to end the constant flow of visitors.

Adolescence intensified all three of Dolly's primary passions. She was becoming more and more serious about singing and songwriting; she was becoming more and more interested in sex; and she was increasingly focused on the private relationship with God that has been a source of her strength in her adult life.

For the sibling-surrounded Dolly, the abandoned chapel near the Parton's land had become the only place where she could find the privacy she needed to sing her own songs, to pray her own prayers, and to muse over the mystery of her emerging sexuality. Sex was there, for sure: young people had drawn more or less accurate anatomical diagrams on the chapel walls and young couples had used it as a meeting place—the rubble on the floor included condom wrappers.

Dolly was twelve years old when suddenly one day it seemed to her as if all three forces—music, sex, and God—were part of one grand design. "As I prayed in earnest," she says, "I broke through some sort of spirit wall and found God...not as a chastising, bombastic bully, but as a friend I could talk to on a one-to-one basis....Here in this place of seemingly confused images, I had found real truth. I had come to know that it was all right for me to be a sexual being...that it was one of the things God meant for me to be.

"I also knew that my dreams of making music...were not silly childhood ideas but grand real schemes ordained and consecrated by my newfound heavenly father. I was validated. I was sanctified. I was truly reborn....The joy of the truth I

Right: **Dolly at thirteen, about the time she took a bus to Louisiana to make her first record.**

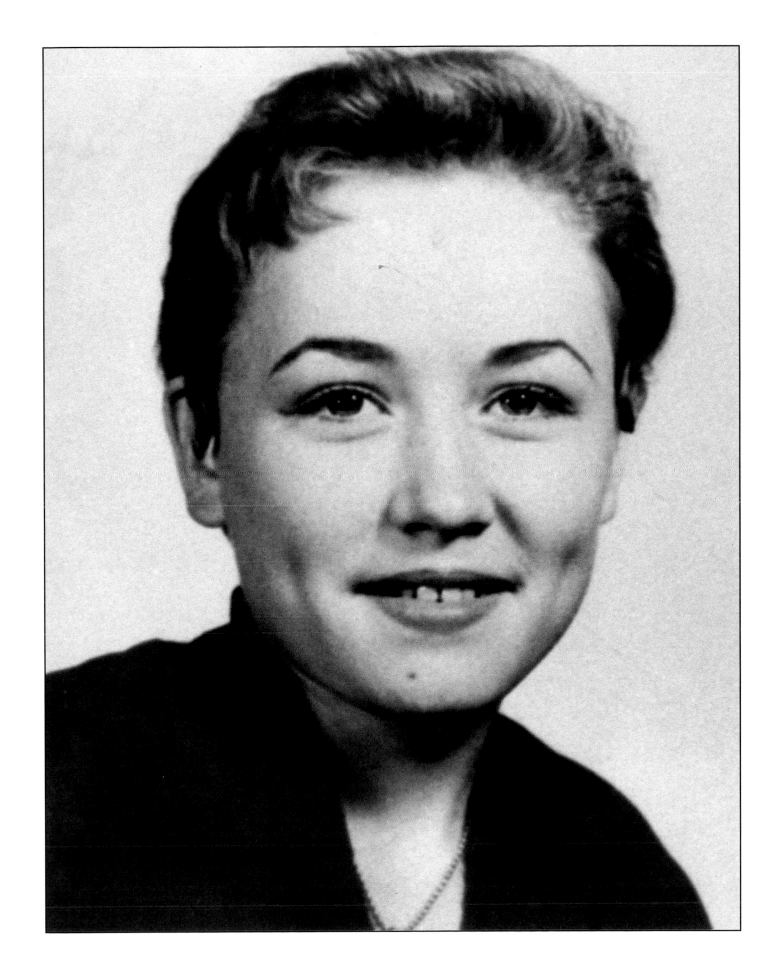

found there is with me to this day. I had found God. I had found Dolly Parton. And I loved them both."

And she knew she was ready to be baptized. The ceremony was performed in the Little Pigeon River by Brother L.D. Smith. In the midst of that intensely religious moment, she was conscious of the reaction of the boys—and men—in the assembled congregation to the sight of her wet dress clinging to her rapidly maturing body.

Not long afterward she made an equally momentous career move: she took an overnight bus trip to Lake Charles, Louisiana, to make her first record. Dolly was given this opportunity because another Owens uncle—Henry, who called himself John Henry III when he tried to break into the music business—was living in Lake Charles and had come to know the people who ran Goldband Records there. While Uncle Bill was visiting Henry in Lake Charles,

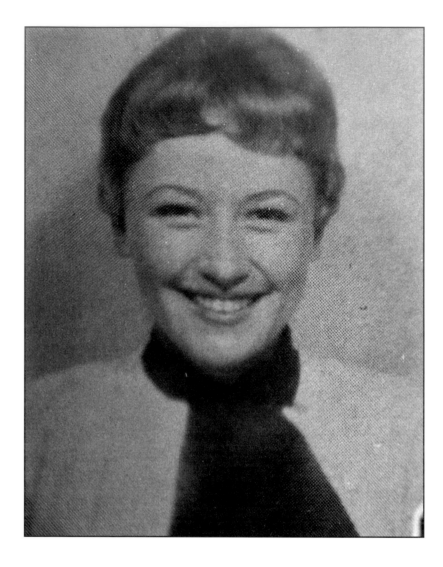

the two decided that Dolly was ready to record and told her parents to send her down.

It was out of the question for a child her age to make the trip alone, but Robert and Avie Lee couldn't possibly leave the farm and the other children. So the family elected Grandma Rena Owens to accompany Dolly.

Neither the grandmother nor her granddaughter had ever been out of Tennessee and the trip was not without its traumas. At one point, the two came out of a bathroom at a rest stop and couldn't recognize their bus among all those in the parking lot. Finally, however, they arrived safely in Lake Charles. The next day Dolly recorded "Puppy Love" at the Goldband Recording Studios, which she herself and Uncle Bill had written, and "Girl Left Alone," by Uncle Bill and Aunt Dorothy Jo Hope.

There was one other thrilling event in Lake Charles: Dolly met her "first real love," Johnny Shuler, the son of the owner of Goldband Records. Although nothing came of the romance, Dolly remembers Johnny as a wonderful kisser. Barely past puberty, she already had enough kissing experience to know when someone was good at it. "Puppy Love" got some airplay and Dolly was on her

Opposite: **Dolly at sixteen, looking more like a typical high-school sophomore than a future star.** *Above:* **Goldband Recording Studios in Lake Charles, Louisiana, where Dolly cut her first record. On the left is Golband owner Eddie Shuler, whose son, Johnny, was Dolly's "first real love."**

way. At thirteen she was still too young to have a clear vision of where she was headed—but her Owens uncles knew. The Cas Walker appearances were now bringing Dolly a munificent sixty dollars a show, but Uncle Bill and Uncle Henry had their sights set on more: namely, Nashville. Dolly and Uncle Bill got in his car and drove halfway across the state—a much less intimidating trip distancewise than the one to Lake Charles, though the goal was even more awe-inspiring: they were heading to the Grand Ole Opry. Dolly's success wasn't immediate; she and her uncles took many trips to Nashville, sleeping in the car at night and hanging around outside the Opry during the day. Because Dolly was still in high school, she could only pursue her career on weekends and school breaks. On one of these trips, Dolly got to meet country giant Johnny Cash, when Uncle Bill introduced him to thirteen-year-old Dolly by the Grand Ole Opry stage door. By Dolly's account she was almost stunned speechless by Cash's raw magnetism, but she managed to blurt out, "Oh, Mister Cash, I've just got to sing on *The Grand Ole Opry.*"

Dolly's Friends Carl & Pearl Butler
"Down on Music Row"

There are few who come to Nashville "sleepy, hungry, tired, [and] dirty" and knock on doors in Music Row until they become, like Dolly, household names. But there are many who arrive the same way only to slink away a few months later into a cold Nashville dawn, heading home or somewhere else, giving up their dreams of stardom.

And then there are those who make it to the middle level of the Nashville pyramid, forging solid careers in country as small-label singers and *Grand Ole Opry*

regulars, but who never become stars or even headliners—the singers and songwriters no one outside of the country world ever hears of. Their numbers are larger than those of country's great names, and smaller than its abject failures. Among them were Dolly's friends and early mentors, honky-tonker Carl Butler and his wife, Pearl.

The Butlers were friends of Dolly's Uncle Bill Owens, Avie Lee Parton's brother, who was himself a lifelong Nashville hopeful. When Uncle Bill got ten-year-old Dolly her first singing job on *The Cas Walker Show* in Knoxville, it was the Butlers who often put her up overnight after the show. Carl was a regular on *The Grand Ole Opry* by then, but he and Pearl hadn't yet started performing together.

Like Dolly, the Butlers were native Tennesseans. Carl was born in 1927 in Knoxville, where he learned to pick guitar listening to the *Opry* and the other country music that surrounded him. Pearl was born in Nashville in

I got into Nashville early,
Sleepy, hungry, tired, dirty
And on the steps of RCA
I ate a stale sweet roll.

"Down on Music Row"–Dolly Parton

1930 and also played guitar and sang as a matter of course. But in the 1940s and 1950s, the country music field was dominated by men; Carl went professional at twelve, but Pearl never dreamed of a musical career.

Carl's debut was at a local square dance. By the time he graduated from high school, he was working steadily, singing and playing on radio programs and at barn dances. In 1948 he joined *The Grand Ole Opry;* not long afterward, he cut his first record for Capitol. (He switched to Columbia a few years later.) When honky-tonk burst onto the scene, he found his niche, writing his own songs like "Crying My Heart Out over You" and "If Teardrops Were Pennies" (the latter co-written with banjo great Earl Scruggs and later recorded by Dolly and Porter Wagoner). Country luminaries including Scruggs, Roy Acuff, and Bill Monroe recorded his songs, and throughout the 1950s, he held his place in what could be called the top of the second rank. In 1961, he recorded his biggest hit to that point, "Honky-Tonkitis."

Honky-tonk was fading from the country scene, however, and if Carl hadn't found a new specialty, his career might have foundered. Luckily, he had one close at hand. He and Pearl had always sung together at home and at family gatherings, and everyone had loved their harmonies; in 1962, they decided to record his latest song together. "Don't Let Me Cross Over" made the country Top Ten, and a disk jockey poll chose the Butlers as the

Number One New Vocal Duo of 1963. They joined *The Grand Ole Opry* as a team at just about the same time Dolly started appearing regularly on the show.

The Butlers continued to record together through the 1960s and performed throughout the 1970s. During the later years of their career together, they adopted the Salvation Army's rehabilitation program as a cause and in 1979 received the organization's Meritorious Service Award. Dolly counted the Butlers among her close friends all their lives. Pearl died in 1988; Carl in 1992.

But it wasn't to be that easy. It took many more trips to Nashville, more sleeping in the car—or, occasionally, at the home of the Butlers, who were by then living in Nashville—more badgering of the Butlers and everyone else they knew who was remotely connected in the music business. Finally, one night, another friend—a Cajun singer named Jimmy C. Newman—yielded to Dolly's pleading and gave her his slot on the show; she was introduced by Johnny Cash himself. Dolly got three encores. When the huge Grand Ole Opry audience applauded her, she saw her path lying before her, brightly lit in the stagelights. In 1961 she and Uncle Bill signed a publishing contract with Tree Music, and in 1962—when she was sixteen—she cut her second record, this time for Mercury: "It May Not Kill Me (But It's Sure Gonna Hurt)," which she had writ-

ten with her uncles Bill and John Henry. High school was fast becoming irrelevant to Dolly. She had always been an ardent learner, but, as with so many other things, always in her own way. The subjects taught in school held little interest for her. Now that she saw success in Nashville just a couple of steps ahead of her, she was starting to see little need for anything she might learn in school.

Nor was her social life particularly engrossing. She has sometimes described herself as not particularly popular among her peers; other times she's said, "I was the most popular girl in school, but in the wrong way. I wore tight clothes and told dirty jokes." Other than her friendship with Judy Ogle—with whom she played the drums in the high school marching band—

there was little to hold her in school.

But Dolly—and, perhaps more to the point, Avie Lee—was determined that she would finish school. "I just wanted to prove I could," she says, and she was the first in her family to do so. Eagerly anticipating the end of her part-time status as a singer, she nevertheless joined the rest of her class on its senior trip to the World's Fair in New York City in the spring of 1964. For one magic moment, she thought the sign on Broadway that said "Hello, Dolly!" was meant for her; then she realized it was only advertising a musical. But the trip gave Dolly a much broader look at the world she was deter-

Opposite: **At fourteen, Dolly was pounding the Nashville pavements with Uncle Bill Owens, looking for an open door.** *Right:* **At seventeen she was already a veteran performer.**

mined to make her name in. Finally, June arrived, and with it her moment of liberation: Graduation Day. During the ceremony, the graduates related their plans as they received their diplomas. While others spoke of getting married and raising families, Dolly announced, "I'm going to Nashville to become a star."

Everyone laughed, but the next morning she was on the bus with all her worldly goods: three shopping bags jammed full of clothes and songs and her guitar.

Left: **The new incarnation of Nashville's The Grand Ole Opry, a far cry from the original, which was housed in the nineteenth-century Ryman Auditorium.** *Right:* **Dolly's senior-class photo, taken not long before she got on a Nashville-bound bus "to become a star."**

CHAPTER THREE

Nashville Grit

1964 — 1967

$\mathcal{A}$ few days after her arrival in Nashville, Dolly wrote home, "Don't worry because I've got a job on an early morning TV show and a couple of people that might record one of the songs I wrote...." Of course she was exaggerating. The reality was a little less heartening. Dolly didn't yet have a job, and she was bitterly homesick: "I even missed being peed on," she later said.

She did get some singing spots on one or two local shows; Ralph Emery and Eddie Hill were the hosts of two early-morning shows she appeared on. Mostly, however, she was scraping by like hundreds of other hopefuls in Nashville. Living on her meager savings, her equally meager singing earnings, and part-time baby-sitting jobs, she stretched every dollar as far as she could. Hunger drove her to embarrassing expedients. She discovered that the people who could afford to stay in the Nashville hotels put out their room-service trays in the corridors, often with a meal's worth of food for a hungry person left over. And ("I'm not proud of this," she says now) she went "shopping" in supermarkets, eating packaged food in the aisles before she reached the checkout counter. The next time she went home for a visit, she was noticeably thinner; when her parents asked why, she told them she was dieting.

Becoming a star was turning out to be much harder than she thought it would be. Pioneers like Kitty Wells, Patsy Cline, and Loretta Lynn had made room for

Previous Photo: **Dolly the year she moved to Nashville, with guitarist Larry Mathis and banjo player Bud Brewster.**
Opposite: **A poster advertising one of her earliest solo appearances.**

I N   P E R S O N

I N   P E R S O N

DOLLY PARTON
OAK GROVE NIGHT CLUB
ON THE ASHEVILLE HIGHWAY
Also—FRANK ROBERTS ☆ TOMMY DICKENS

women in the formerly exclusive good old boys' club that country music had been, and Nashville was teeming with female talent; Tammy Wynette, only a few years older than Dolly, was just becoming a star.

But if her big break was eluding her, she was nevertheless slowly forging ahead—always carrying Uncle Bill along with her. The two of them signed a recording and publishing contract with Fred Foster of Combine Publishing and Monument Records. Foster thought that Dolly would do better as a rockabilly singer rather than sticking to straight country and tried to shape her into one. He got her appearances on *American Bandstand* and at a jukebox convention in Chicago, but except for allowing Dolly to experience her first airplane flight, rockabilly wasn't taking her very far.

Something else was going on in her life that was keeping her career frustrations from overwhelming her: a romance that has since become a country legend. One day, she was drinking a Coke on the sidewalk outside the Wishy Washy laundromat near her Nashville apartment, passing the time as her laundry tumbled dry inside. She was wearing, she says, a red outfit that maximized her spectacular charms, and a handsome young asphalt contractor named Carl Dean drove by. He waved at the pretty young woman in red, she waved back—and their hormones took it from there. (Some of Dolly's accounts of that meeting make it even more legendary by placing it on the very day after she arrived in Nashville.) Although he was a Nashville native, Carl Thomas Dean had no interest in the music business. The son of Tennesseans Edgar Henry and Virginia Bates Dean, Carl was twenty-two and working

Opposite: **A rare photo of the limelight-shunning Carl Dean, Dolly's husband since 1966.** *Right:* **Dolly was billed as a "local singer" in this 1966 publicity shot.**

for his father's paving business the day he drove by the Wishy Washy. Twelve years later, Dolly told an interviewer that she was attracted to Carl's "honesty," his "decency," his "earthiness," and the "way he lets me be free."

Over the next two years, they spent as much time together as possible. Dolly was traveling frequently to sing on radio and television programs around the country, and Carl was in the National Guard, but if they were in Nashville, they were together. Carl wasn't a man who was free with his feelings and Dolly waited and waited for Carl to tell her he loved her. One day, in a decidedly unromantic manner, Carl sighed, "Either you move to [my] side of town, or we get married."

Dolly picked the latter—but when she agreed to marry Carl, she wasn't talking about a conventional marriage. Years later, she repeated exactly what she said to Carl, along with that "yes": "I love to cook, but I'm gonna make enough money for somebody else to cook. It's not gonna be my duty and it's not gonna be my job and I damn sure ain't gonna clean house and I'm not washing no dishes because I'm not ruining my fingernails. I'm gonna write songs and I'm gonna sing." And, she added, "I'll be gone most of the time."

Apparently, that was good enough for Carl. On May 29, 1966, he and Dolly and Avie Lee ("I wanted to have my mother at my wedding," Dolly says) drove through most of Tennessee to Ringgold, Georgia, a marriage mill across the state line from Chattanooga. But when they got there, they discovered that they could be married on the spot only by a justice of the peace, but that they would have to wait until the next day to have the ceremony performed in a church.

Because of the important role God played in her life, Dolly wanted a religious wedding, so back they drove to Nashville, still unmarried. They returned the next day; this time they were successful. A Ringgold minister married Dolly and Carl on May 30, 1966. They drove back to Nashville but the newlyweds had a very short wedding night: Dolly had to work on a radio show at the crack of dawn the next morning.

Country singers tend to marry early and often, yet, thirty years later, it looks as if the Parton-Dean union is a keeper. It has withstood stresses that have driven many other show-business marriages to court, including Dolly's frequent appearances in the tabloids and her virtually constant traveling. (Once, asked whether she believes in living together before marriage, she quipped, "I don't believe in living together *after* marriage!")

But stardom and its costs were still in the future, though not as far away as they may have looked the day Dolly and Carl got married. That same year, Dolly sang an uncredited backup on a song she and Uncle Bill had written, "Put It off Till Tomorrow." This Bill Phillips record was chosen as the BMI Song of the Year for 1966, and country promoters and disk jockeys across the country wanted to know whose was the

Opposite: **A headshot of Dolly taken for Moeller Talent.**

Left: Porter with Norma Jean Beasler, whose resignation from *The Porter Wagoner Show* gave Dolly her big break in 1967. Dolly went onstage a "dumb blonde" and left seven years later as one of country's biggest stars—but first she had to win over Norma Jean's fans. *Right:* In an effort to make her more marketable, Monument Records tried to promote Dolly as a rockabilly singer. The effort failed.

lovely voice on backup. More to the point, perhaps, it convinced Combine Records owner Fred Foster that Dolly could make it as a country singer after all.

In 1967, when Dolly was twenty-one years old, Foster recorded her covering Curly Putnam's "Dumb Blonde"—a song that seemed tailor-made for her. The flip side featured Dolly singing her own song, "Something Fishy." The record made country's Top Twenty-Five. Monument put her on an album, *Hello, I'm Dolly*, and Uncle Bill and Dolly founded their own music publishing company called Owepar, a combination of the first three letters of each of their last names. Dolly also signed with Moeller Talent and acquired Don Warden as a manager. She released another hit single, "Just Because I'm a Woman." Then, at the end of that summer, Dolly got the break she was waiting for.

Norma Jean Beasler (her stage name was Norma Jean), the lead singer on veteran country star Porter Wagoner's immensely popular syndicated television program, *The Porter Wagoner Show*, decided to quit. By that time, Dolly had sung on virtually every country music radio and television show that came out of Nashville, and many in other parts of the country. In addition to Emery's and Hill's, she had appeared on *The Midday Merry-Go-Round*, *The Bill Anderson Show*, and *The Wilburn Brothers Show*, to name a few. Nashville insiders all knew the pretty twenty-one-year-old songwriter with the sweet voice and the gorgeous figure. Yet Dolly and Carl were still living in their little Nashville apartment. When Wagoner called Dolly and said, "I want you to be my new girl singer," the offer to perform on his television show sounded heaven-sent.

This opportunity would carry her to performing heaven—and bring with it just a little bit of hell on earth.

Dolly's First Partner, Porter Wagoner

Like his most famous singing partner, Porter Wagoner was a child of America's farmland—not native to the stony farms of the Eastern mountains, as Dolly was, but to those of the broad fertile plain of southern Missouri, just west of the Mississippi River.

Wagoner was born to a farming family in West Plains, Missouri, in 1930 (or 1927—sources differ). His childhood was shadowed by his father's disabling arthritis, which forced young Porter to shoulder more than his share of the farmwork. Yet somehow he found the time to learn to pick guitar from the country music of the 1930s.

As a young man, Porter went to work in a local grocery store; his picking and strumming in front of the store got him a spot promoting the store on a local radio station. In his early twenties, his talents first won him his own show at KWTO in the big city—Springfield—and then the attention of 1950s country giant Red Foley (who may have been the first country performer to record in Nashville). In 1955, Wagoner joined Foley's *Ozark Jamboree*, broadcasting out of Springfield. He remained with Foley for four years, meanwhile starting a recording career under contract with RCA (later, he would bring the young Dolly Parton to RCA as well). His early country Top Ten hits included "What Would You Do if Jesus Came to Your House?" and "Satisfied Mind."

In 1957, he joined *The Grand Ole Opry*, but by then it was clear that his talent needed a broader stage; he already knew that his gifts included songwriting as well as performing. In 1960, still in his early thirties, he founded his own band, the Wagonmasters—with young Norma Jean Beasler as his lead "girl singer"—and started *The Porter Wagoner Show*. A virtually unbroken string of Top Five and Top Ten hits followed, including "Misery Loves Company," "Green Green Grass of Home," and "Skid Row Joe."

Ironically, however, it was as Dolly Parton's mentor that Wagoner got his greatest fame. Dolly joined his show in 1967; she was twenty-one and Wagoner was nearing forty, but by the time she left him in 1974, the protégée had far outshone the mentor. Wagoner's greatest record sales came from his dozen-plus duet albums with Dolly; they included 1969's *Always, Always* and 1970's *Porter Wayne and Dolly Rebecca*. Throughout the Dolly years, he continued to record both solo and with other singers, including the country singer's country singer, Skeeter Davis, and the gospel group the Blackwood Brothers. Several of the albums with the Blackwood Brothers won Grammys, including *Grand Ole Gospel* in 1966 and *In Gospel Country* in 1969. (During the years Dolly worked with Porter, she never recorded with anyone else, though she made many solo records.)

Although their partnership brought both of them so much, Parton and Wagoner actually had very different musical styles (though it might be more accurate to say that Dolly's range was far broader than Porter's). He was an old-fashioned, straight-ahead country man, influenced by bluegrass and gospel; Dolly was part of the new, pop-influenced Nashville, and though the twain did meet for a rich and productive seven years, it was inevitable that they would go their separate ways.

The split was rancorous, and Porter sued Dolly for three million dollars. In one final incongruous note, many of Porter's later hits were from duet albums with Dolly; they had recorded so much together that RCA was able to continue releasing their records well into the 1980s.

Onstage at *The Porter Wagoner Show*, Porter takes the foreground with Dolly just a little behind him.

CHAPTER FOUR

The Porter Years

1967 — 1974

*P*orter Wagoner's star performer, Norma Jean, was pushing thirty in 1967, and wanted to quit the show and get married. Born Norma Jean Beasler in Wellston, Oklahoma, she had begun performing on radio and television in Oklahoma City in 1956 and had become a regular on *Ozark Jubilee* in 1956. In 1960, she had come to Nashville, and Wagoner had "discovered" her, as he would Dolly seven years later. After recording for a while with Columbia, she moved to RCA in 1963; the next year, her "Let's Go All the Way" made country's Top Ten. She had other hits over the next few years, but being Wagoner's "girl singer" may have begun to chafe; by all accounts, he wasn't an easy man to work for.

In 1965, Norma Jean started talking about "semi-retiring," and in 1967 finally worked up enough courage to walk away from the show, providing Dolly with a golden opportunity. On September 5 of that year, Dolly made her debut on Wagoner's program. In her words, her time with Porter constituted both "the hardest and worst" and "the most prosperous, productive, and growth-filled" years of her life.

It started badly. As soon as Wagoner introduced Dolly, members of the live audience that had known and loved her predecessor called out, "We want Norma Jean!" They quieted down some when Dolly sang, but they didn't warm up to her enough to give her the welcome she wanted. Nor did the debut program see the end of the audience's dissatisfaction: although Dolly was now appearing on every show, someone was always asking for Norma Jean.

Previous Photo: **Dolly with the rest of the cast of *The Porter Wagoner Show.*** *Right:* **Dolly in 1968, the year she and Porter won their first Country Music Association award.**

In October, still unhappy with her progress with Wagoner's audiences, Dolly nevertheless signed a recording contract with his label, RCA. Dolly and Wagoner then put out a cover of folksinger Tom Paxton's lovely "The Last Thing on My Mind." Sevier County declared a Dolly Parton Day that included a performance by Dolly on the steps of the county courthouse. Early in 1968, RCA released the first of what would be Dolly and Wagoner's dozen-plus albums together, *Just Between You and Me.* The album won the 1968 Country Music Award for best duet of the year, and suddenly Dolly and Wagoner were a hit combination. Finally, the Wagoner audiences loved and accepted her.

Wagoner was paying Dolly sixty thousand dollars a year, far more money than she and Carl had ever seen before. They moved to a bigger house in Nashville—one that several of her siblings would come to call home for a while. And starting in 1969, Dolly's childhood friend Judy Ogle would come and go over the course of the next decade, staying on for years at a time to help Dolly in various capacities.

As well as recording with Wagoner, Dolly was putting out her own records steadily; more and more, they incorporated her own perspective, proudly blue-collar (as in "Coat of Many Colors" and "In the Good Old Days When Times Were Bad") and subversively feminist (as in "Dumb Blonde," "Just Because I'm a Woman," and the prostitute-friendly "My Blue Ridge Mountain Boy"). In 1970, her cover of the country classic "Mule Skinner Blues" topped the country charts and was nominated for a Grammy, and her own song "Joshua" also came close to the #1 spot. In 1971 she got her first country #1 with one of her own songs, "Jolene," and the same year "Coat of Many Colors" made the Top Five. Somewhere in that time, she and Porter recorded "Daddy Was an Old-Time Preacher Man," the song she and her aunt, Dorothy Jo Hope, had written about Grandpa Jake Owens. That was a hit, too. No question about it, Dolly was well on her way to fulfilling her Graduation Day promise and she was only twenty-five years old.

But success had its price. Her schedule was a punishing one; it wasn't unusual for her to do fifteen performances in twenty days. In 1971, she took her whole family to Florida for a vacation, intending to send everyone home and go off alone with Carl at the end of it, but the second half never happened— something came up, as it often did.

Dolly Parton

59

Above: **Dolly Parton and Bob Nyles listen to Dolly's newest single, "Jolene."**

Left: **Country Music Association awards night in Nashville, 1970: (left to right) Roy Clarke, Merle Haggard, Dolly, and Porter.**

And there were increasing tensions with Wagoner. Affectionate by nature, Dolly says she hates to fight; Porter, on the other hand, "liked to quarrel and argue and shout." Their relationship was stormy enough to give rise to the suspicion in many minds that they were more than colleagues; the fact that Porter persisted in buying her diamonds—though she could well afford to buy them for herself—did nothing to quiet the wagging tongues. Dolly herself refuses to say either way, but then, she refuses to admit or deny affairs with anyone else, either. (She does say that Carl wasn't the first man in her life, but won't say if he was the last, only insisting that one of the keys to the success of their marriage has been his great tolerance for all the exigencies of her career.)

Whether or not Wagoner was her lover, there is no doubt that he saw himself as her Svengali. She says he tried to dictate what she sang, where she sang it, and what she wore to sing in; offstage he also attempted to control how and with whom she spent her time, and had edged Fred Foster and her Owens uncles to the periphery of her life. (He had long since bought into Owepar Publishing, for instance.) It's unclear just how much of a hand he had in shaping the image that became her trademark: It was "not far," in the words of one critic, "from that of Diamond Lil [Mae West's sultry character in the 1933 film *She Done Him Wrong*]: a mountainous, curlicued, bleached-blonde wig, lots of makeup, and outfits that accentuate her quite astonishing hourglass figure."

She stuck it out with Wagoner for seven years—exactly as many as Norma Jean had given him. Dolly had realized, however, that the sixty thousand dollars a year Wagoner was paying her came out to only three hundred dollars a night for every night she worked—and that she could probably make much more on her own. One day in 1974, alone in her car, she found herself composing as she drove, writing the song about deliverance that became "Light of a Clear Blue Morning."

Perhaps, too, she had already had a glimpse of broader musical horizons without Wagoner. "It was time to go," she recalls.

By 1968, Dolly was well on the way to becoming the Dolly Parton the world knows and loves, but she still wasn't flaunting her figure as she did later.

Dolly Parton, Songwriter

New York Times writer John Rockwood praised "the sheer quality of [Dolly's] songs" and called them "haunting in their asymmetrical freshness." Atlanta pop music critic Gene Guerero went further, calling Dolly, "along with Merle Haggard, one of this generation's most important songwriters."

Dolly's looks, charm, and humor may have won the hearts of country—and pop—audiences, but it is her songwriting talent that has won the respect of the music world. Dolly began creating songs before she was old enough to write them down; she was barely seven years old when she started dictating her songs to her mother, Avie Lee, a musician and the daughter of a musician. Since her childhood, Dolly has written "hundreds and hundreds" of songs (three thousand of them, she told one reporter).

"I've written more than most writers do," she says. "It's just so easy.... Most people sit down and smoke a pipe, but I just sit down and pick up a piece of paper."

Like many of country's greatest songwriters, Dolly is able to capture in song the experiences and lives of hard-working blue-collar people, the kind who still make up the core of her audience. From childhood on, she wrote about the world of her origins, about what she saw and what she knew, whether it was love as she then understood it or the hard facts of life in Tennessee. Her first record, made when she was in her early teens, was "Puppy Love," and many of her earliest hits were based on incidents or people in her life. "In the Good Old Days When Times Were Bad" (1969) is a straightforward description of the struggles of working-class life. "Daddy Was an Old-Time Preacher Man" (co-written with her aunt Dorothy Jo Hope) is a portrait of her grandfather, "Rev." Jake Owens, while "Jolene" (1974) describes a young woman from Sevierville. "Coat of Many Colors" (1971), her second song to hit country's Top Five, is an account of a memorable moment in her childhood when the children in her school made fun of her for wearing a patchwork jacket her mother had sewn from old clothes, and "Down on Music Row" is a narration of the hardships of breaking into the music business.

One measure of Dolly's songwriting skills is the number of big names—in and out of country—who have produced hits with her songs. Maria Muldaur covered "My Tennessee Mountain Home"; Emmylou Harris sang "Coat of Many Colors"; Olivia

Oh, these northern nights are dreary,
And my southern heart is weary...
Appalachian memories keep me strong.

"Appalachian Memories" –Dolly Parton, 1983

Newton-John recorded "Jolene." In 1994, Whitney Houston's powerhouse cover of Dolly's 1974 "I Will Always Love You" broke all previous records by staying at #1 on the pop charts for fourteen weeks.

Dolly started writing less and less about her early years and her Tennessee home. The little girl from Pigeon Forge had found new ideas to play with; Dolly's repertoire was expanding. As early as 1977, she had shocked country listeners with "Here You Come Again," a deliberate—and successful—attempt to cross over into pop, and that same year "Light of a Clear Blue Morning" climbed higher in pop than it did on the country charts. She insisted she wasn't leaving country: "I'm taking it with me," she said. In 1980, she penned "9 to 5," the assertively class-conscious title song for her first movie, and in 1983, "Appalachian Memories" paid elo-

Dolly singing to a hometown audience on Dolly Parton Day in Sevierville, 1970.

quent tribute to the country she was born in.

As important as writing remains to her, however, Dolly's other ventures—and her status as a pop icon—loom larger and larger in her life, and writing has come to take up less of her time. And, after all, she no longer has to write for a living; she's no longer the hungry teenager who got on a bus with a paper bag full of songs to make it big in Nashville.

Yet she still has what it takes. Critics called 1987's "Wildflowers" one of the loveliest songs she's ever written. In 1991, she had a sassy hit with "Romeo" (the video also featured Billy Ray Cyrus). And whether ultimately her fame will rest more on her performances, her persona, or her songs will depend on how she will shape her career in the future, which promises to be prosperous—and to take turns in new directions—for a long time to come.

CHAPTER FIVE

On Her Own

1974 — 1980

*A*fter leaving Porter, Dolly formed her own band. Not surprisingly, about half of it was comprised of her siblings, including Rachel, the baby of the family, then about fifteen. With somewhat less than her usual imagination—but absolutely typical clan loyalty—Dolly called it the Traveling Family Band.

She had a big hit with her own "I Will Always Love You" (years later a megahit when Whitney Houston covered it in the movie *The Bodyguard*), and, backed by her family, she went on tour. In September 1974, Dolly and the band appeared in New York City's Felt Forum, a daring step given New York's lack of interest in country music at the time. Even though reviewer John Rockwell of *The New York Times* called the appearance "a commercial failure," he praised Dolly as an "impressive artist" and gave her full marks for her beautiful singing and for "the sheer quality of her songs."

It was ten years and a summer since Dolly's Graduation Day pledge to go to Nashville and become a star, and if she wasn't quite nationally famous yet, she certainly was among Music City's rising stars. By now, she was friends with some of country's luminaries, like guitar great Chet Atkins and the up-and-coming Mac Davis.

Previous Photo: **A thousand-watt smile. In 1975, Dolly was finally on her own, following the turmoil of the Porter years.** *Opposite:* **Dolly giving a free concert on the steps of New York's City Hall on August 21, 1978, after her August 22 show at the Palladium sold out, leaving hundreds of eager fans ticketless. According to police reports, the City Hall appearance outdrew one by then-President Jimmy Carter.**

But for all her new friendships, she hadn't completely shaken off Porter Wagoner. Perhaps she didn't really want to. Wagoner had been her mentor; he had made her famous. They had been, if not lovers, closer than lovers in many ways, and Dolly—who says she still loves Wagoner—is not one to let go easily of any tie she has made.

In any case, Wagoner was reluctant to let her go, and the break was anything but clean. Before long, he had sued her for three million dollars on the grounds that, having made her a star, "he was entitled to a portion of my earnings for life," says Dolly.

Disastrous as it seemed, the situation with Porter actually brought something good into Dolly's life. Mac Davis recommended that she turn her career over to the Los Angeles megamanagement firm of Katz, Gallin, and Morey, and she's been with Sandy Gallin ever since.

Above: **Dolly and up-and-coming country-pop singer Mac Davis. After her stint with Porter Wagoner, Mac referred Dolly to Sandy Gallin, still her manager today.** *Opposite:* **Dolly trying out the western side of Country and Western.**

The tabloids have suggested that they were together in more ways than one; she and Gallin have shared a New York pied-à-terre that some of the scandal sheets have alleged is also a love nest. That's one rumor that Dolly has more or less firmly denied, but Gallin has definitely joined her family. Along with her blood kin and Judy Ogle—and, of course, Carl—Gallin is one of the steadiest and most loved figures in Dolly's world.

One of the first things Gallin did was help Dolly settle Wagoner's suit. The terms of the settlement bar Dolly from giving out details, but she has hinted that she spent the next several years paying him something in the neighborhood of one million dollars.

Much to her dismay, Dolly's Traveling Family Band didn't work out. She gave it two years and then put together a new band, without so many siblings. The press, she complains now, "made it sound like I had fired my family. I did not fire my family. " The rearrangement, she says, was by mutual consent.

Left: **Dolly's sense of humor always comes across when she performs.**

Right: **As her solo career skyrocketed, Dolly searched for her own image. This 1977 RCA publicity shot shows her looking western, buxom, and brash.**

By 1976—at about the same time she finally severed all her business ties to Wagoner—she was big enough to rate a major story in *The New York Times Magazine*, possibly because she was venturing into another controversial career area. Under Gallin's management, her sound was becoming just a little more pop, and perhaps just a little less country. Her 1977 hit, "Here You Come Again," was her first million-copy selling record—and her first to cross over to the pop charts in a big way. It hit the #3 spot, and the country world howled at the crossover, believing that Dolly—by then a Nashville icon—

Stella Parton
Dolly's Singing Sister

Dolly may be the most successful with her family's musical gifts so far, but she certainly has no monopoly on them.

Music flowed from the Parton children like water. Several of Dolly's older siblings also sang and wrote. All four of the youngest—her brother Randy; the twins, Floyd and Freida; and baby sister Rachel—along with Dolly's cousin Dwight, performed in the short-lived Traveling Family Band that Dolly formed when she struck out on her own after leaving Porter Wagoner in 1974. But of all the Parton children, only Stella had a solid career independent of her famous big sister.

Three years younger than Dolly, Stella is the sixth of Robert and Avie Lee's children. Born in 1949, Stella showed her talent so early that at the age of six, she joined Dolly on a local radio show for her singing debut. (They sang the Louvin Brothers' "Because She Is My Mother.") By the time Stella was seventeen, she was singing in local clubs.

Dolly was in Nashville then; that year—1966—was the year Dolly's voice first drew attention as the uncredited backup on Bill Phillips' recording of "Put It off Till Tomorrow." But it wasn't clear exactly what Stella's niche would be. She drifted around the country world, going to Washington and then Texas before returning to Nashville. She recorded on a couple of small labels— Royal American, Music City—and then formed a gospel group called Stella Carroll and the Gospel Carrolls.

In 1975, Stella's career got a boost through a minor country scandal: Anglo-Australian pop singer Olivia Newton-John won the Country Music Award for Best Female Vocalist (she had just released "Let It Be Me") and country fans and performers alike roared their protests. Stella penned an "Ode to Olivia" defending Newton-John's status as a country singer; suddenly she was back in Nashville and back in country. Stella refined her own distinct image when audiences began to enjoy the fact that she had as many hats as Dolly had wigs.

Like her big sister, Stella is a songwriter as well as a singer. Recording on the Country Soul and Blues label, Stella had one country hit in 1975 and another the next year: "I Want to Hold You in My Heart" and "I Want to Hold You with My Dreams Tonight," respectively. In 1977, Stella signed with Elektra records and over the next several years had a steady stream of

Top Twenty country hits, including "Danger of a Stranger," "Standard Lie Number One," "Four Little Words," "Stormy Weather," and "Steady as the Rain."

Not long after Dolly went to Hollywood, Stella decided to try acting, too. She succeeded as the madam in the national tour of the musical *Best Little Whorehouse In Texas*. (It was the same role Dolly had played onscreen.)

Stella remains a country favorite, still touring and writing songs. In 1996, she released *A Woman's Touch*, her first album in several years; she wrote most of the songs on it herself, but one—"Smooth Talker"—was co-written with yet another of the singing-songwriting Partons, little brother Floyd.

Stella Parton with singer Mark Hardwick, who sang "The Night Dolly Parton Was Almost Mine" in Broadway's country musical *Pump Boys and Dinettes*.

Left: A Grand Ole Opry appearance in 1979—a far cry from the terrified teenager who had debuted there almost two decades earlier. *Right:* Dolly showing a sensitive, intimate side.

was abandoning them for the wider world of pop. "I'm not leaving country," she told them. "I'm taking it with me."

And take it she did—across the United States and beyond. In 1977 she appeared on *The Tonight Show* for the first of what would be hundreds of late-night network guest slots, and the next year she was certified as a big-time star when famed interviewer Barbara Walters included Dolly in one of her

specials. Dolly's first nationally syndicated television show, *Dolly*, lasted a couple of years until it became more trouble than it was worth. On it, however, she accomplished much that she was proud of, most memorably the night she shared the stage for the first time with country-pop star Linda Ronstadt and queen of country-rock Emmylou Harris. (The three would reunite a decade later for the spectacularly successful *Trio* album.)

Now, several years after she left Wagoner, she found a new man to sing with who was more amenable to a part-time partnership: country superstar Kenny Rogers. She also took her first European tour at this time.

Linda Ronstadt, Dolly, and Emmylou Harris were good friends for years before they made the *Trio* album.

Dolly was coming into her own, not only as a star, but as a businesswoman. Her enterprises were becoming more lucrative and more far-flung, and she needed an ever-larger staff. But with Carl maintaining the distance from her career that he always had, she needed someone else: one person who would always be at her side, at home or on tour. Just at that juncture, Judy Ogle, who had joined the U.S. Army a few years before, decided to return to Nashville and civilian life. She moved back in with Dolly and Carl and has been on Dolly's staff ever since, as "assistant, valet, hairdresser, makeup artist," and whatever else Dolly needs her to be.

Dolly (left) and her lifelong best friend, Judy Ogle, leaving the Lyceum Theatre in London.

Dolly has made no secret of the fact that on the road she and Judy often share a bed. Though she tends to be coy about her sexual and romantic life, she has persistently denied that she and Judy do anything but sleep and giggle in that bed, just like they did when they were kids thirty years ago in the East Tennessee mountains. (After all, she reminds skeptics, she comes from a world where everyone shares a bed; she had virtually never slept alone until she got to Nashville in 1964.)

By 1980—the year she released an album with country's first female superstar, Kitty Wells—Dolly was at the top, not only of Nashville, but of pop. She, Carl, Judy Ogle and an ever-changing number of Parton siblings were living on an eighty-acre estate outside Nashville called Tara (Dolly has never claimed to be subtle). Her personal and business staff numbered fifty. Like Alexander the Great, she was looking for new worlds to conquer. One strongly beckoned her: Hollywood.

CHAPTER SIX

Hollywood to Dollywood

1980 – 1987

*I*n 1979, on the strength of Dolly's immense popularity, 20th-Century Fox signed her to a nonexclusive three-picture deal; shortly afterward, on the strength of her talent and charm, Jane Fonda chose her to play Doralee Rhodes, one of the three office workers portrayed in *9 to 5*. "I had never met her," Fonda explained, "but...anyone who can write 'Coat of Many Colors' and sing it the way she does has got the stuff to do anything. This [Dolly] was not...the stereotype of a dumb blonde."

Though Dolly was perfectly comfortable in front of cameras—by this time she had been appearing in front of them for twenty years—she had never acted before. "I didn't know exactly what the movies were all about," she told an interviewer later, "so I memorized the whole script. Every part."

Dolly stole the show, right out of the hands of veteran actresses Fonda and Lily Tomlin—and they loved her for it. "She was wonderful," said Tomlin; "she's so quick, so natural, down-to-earth [and] bigger than life." The title song, penned by Dolly, became one of her biggest hits and earned an Academy Award nomination. Before 1980 ended, 20th-Century Fox offered her more than a million dollars to star with Burt Reynolds in the movie musical *Best Little Whorehouse in Texas*. She signed a multimillion-dollar deal for a series of Las Vegas appearances.

Previous Photo: **Fonda, Tomlin, and Dolly with Dabney Coleman, the chauvinist boss on whom they wreak hilarious revenge in** *9 to 5*. *Right:* **The stars of** *9 to 5* **—veteran comic Lily Tomlin, Oscar winner Jane Fonda, and Dolly, who stole every scene she was in.**

Dolly Parton
84

Opposite: **Every time Dolly kissed someone on screen the tabloids blared allegations of real-life affairs. They accused her of romancing Burt Reynolds when she co-starred with him in** *Best Little Whorehouse in Texas...* *Below:* **...and Sylvester Stallone after** *Rhinestone.*

The 1982 release of *Whorehouse* brought her a new set of favorable reviews, and in 1983 her album with Kenny Rogers, *Islands in the Stream*, became a megahit for both stars, with the title song hitting #1 on the pop charts. At thirty-seven, Dolly was at the top of her career: "a one-woman gold rush," as one journalist wrote, "the hottest thing ever to come out of the Great Smoky Mountains."

The tabloids thought she was hot, too. During the filming of *Whorehouse*, they insisted that Dolly and Reynolds were having a romance; a year later, when she shot *Rhinestone* with Sylvester Stallone, the scandal sheets said Stallone was her lover. Insisting that her marriage to Carl was secure enough to withstand the barrage, Dolly's responses were flip and noncommittal. "It could be worse," she quipped once. "They could print the truth about me."

But there was trouble brewing in Dolly's world—big trouble. In January of 1983, Dolly canceled a scheduled concert in Owensboro, Kentucky, announcing to the public that she had received threats on her life. An Owensboro police sergeant told a newspaper that he had personally heard one threatening call. Then she canceled more shows. A spokesperson said that she was hiring a "security consultant," and that she would have no public performances until an investigation was completed. There is no record of anyone being caught or indicted for the threats.

It was clear, however, to anyone who saw her that something was seriously wrong in her world. She was putting on weight; she would add fifty pounds to her five-foot frame before getting her body—and her life—back under control. Dolly looked haunted and ill.

In fact, it was a series of disastrous events that plunged her into a deep depression for an eighteen-month period that she would later describe as the worst in her life. She has since said that a "betrayal"—revelations about her private life by a close associate—and an "affair of the heart" made her overweight and sick. As to the nature of the illness, she has mentioned both an ulcer and "female problems." Dolly had a partial hysterectomy at some point during the crisis. She has also talked about binge eating and grief for the children she had realized she would never have.

Dolly managed, however, to seize one business opportunity that came along during that dark time: the chance to be one of the first country stars with her own theme park. It was the mid-1980s, and theme parks were booming across the United States. Dolly decided she wanted one; by a happy coincidence, the people who ran Silver Dollar City, in Pigeon Forge—forty miles from Knoxville and around the corner from the mountainside cabin where she was born—were looking for new money. "All we had to do was 'Dolly-ize' it," she said ten years later, at a reported cost of seventy million dollars. Dollywood opened in 1985, despite Dolly's personal turmoil.

Yet the depression persisted. Then one morning, as she related long afterward, she stared for a long time at the gun she kept next to her bed. Finally she told herself, "Either you...get past this point in your life, or kill yourself already." As is characteristic of her personality, she summoned the strength and the courage to keep on living. Dolly made a pact with God: "I said, 'Help me pull through this and I'll become a better person.'"

Right: **Dolly's smile hid her mounting depression in 1981.**

A Day in Dollywood

So what can you do in Dolly's theme park?

Well, pretty much the same things you can do in any other— and more. Forty miles from Knoxville and around the corner from Sevierville, Dollywood has expanded considerably in the twelve years since its relatively modest seventy-million-dollar beginnings. As of 1997, you can take any number of rides, including thrillers like the Mountain Slidewinder or old-timey ones like a steam-driven railroad train and an antique-style handcrafted carousel.

You can also dance and listen to music—mostly country, of course. There are performances by megastars from the Grand Ole Opry and other Nashville venues; there are gospel concerts; there are lesser-known traditional singers from the immediate vicinity of the Great Smoky Mountains; and there are specialty performances like a "fabulous '50s" rock and roll show.

Kids can play in a Lego Land, and visitors of all ages can watch local craftspeople create their wares. Some of these people are old family friends, like soapmaker Della Hurst, who pinned Dolly's first diaper on her in the winter of 1946. ("She came and helped," Dolly remembers, "because Momma had a hard time with my birth.") Dollywood is also home to an eagle sanctuary, reportedly the nation's largest assemblage of non-

releaseable bald eagles, that is, wild eagles that have been injured and can't be put back in the wild.

Most of all, however, you can see Dolly, and, as is always the case in Dolly's productions, other Partons in films about her, exhibits from her life and milieu, and occasional appearances by the star herself. There's a Dolly Parton museum in which Dolly's life is recounted via "video reflections and personal mementos selected by Dolly herself." Her brother Randy Parton hosts a musical performance. There's even a movie, *Heartsong,* presenting "the musical story of Dolly's life."

Dollywood has contributed substantially to Dolly's enormous wealth. What it's done for Sevier County, however, has been debated by locals since the park opened. Some claim that by driving property values up, Dollywood has made it harder for them to find affordable homes. Dolly answers that it creates jobs for local people—and that a substantial portion of the park's gross receipts goes back to her charities, particularly the Dollywood Foundation, which encourages at-risk children in Sevier County to stick with their studies and graduate from high school.

One thing is sure: Dolly and Dollywood, between them, have definitely put tiny Pigeon Forge, Tennessee, on the map.

Dolly's

y logo is everywhere in Dollywood, even in the flowerbeds.

Dolly Parton
91

Dolly suspended her career and turned her full attention to getting well. The primary components of her plan were prayer and dieting; together or separately, they worked. As 1986 turned into 1987, Dolly was back. Happy and weighing a diminutive 105 pounds, she broadcast one of her most successful television shows ever, a made-for-TV, partly autobiographical movie called *A Smoky Mountain Christmas.*

Previous Pages: **(left) the grist mill at Dollywood; (right) Dolly presiding over her theme park.** *Opposite:* **As she recovered from the disastrous events of the early '80's, Dolly made a TV movie, *A Smoky Mountain Christmas,* with Lee Majors.** *Right:* **Afterward, she said that prayer—and a pact with God—got her through the bad time.**

CHAPTER SEVEN

The Steel Magnolia

1987 — 1997

*N*ineteen eighty-seven started with a double-barreled flourish. On January 12, Dolly won yet another award, and on January 16—three days before her forty-first birthday—she signed a new recording contract.

Of the two events, the first was by far the more astonishing. *Ms.* magazine honored Dolly as a "Woman of the Year" for 1986, along with South Africa's Winnie Mandela, Maryland Senator Barbara Mikulksi, and *Cagney & Lacey* stars Sharon Gless and Tyne Daly.

Dolly's response was uncharacteristically muted, as if it wasn't quite clear to her what she was doing in that crowd: "I think I make quite a statement as a woman," she said, "because I'm interested in business and I've been managing all my life."

Gloria Steinem, on the other hand, was anything but muted in the January *Ms.* article that gave the reasons for the award. "For creating popular songs about real women, for turning feminine style into humor and power, and for bringing jobs and understanding to the mountain people of Tennessee," Steinem wrote. "People...may be surprised to learn that [Dolly Parton and feminism] go together. In fact, she has crossed musical class lines to bring work, real life, and strong women into a world of pop music usually dominated by unreal romance. She has used her business sense to bring other women and poor people along with her. And her flamboyant style has turned all the devalued symbols of womanliness to her own ends."

Previous Photo: **The new, petite Dolly—happy, healthy and ready to conquer the world.** *Right:* **Even the feminists succumbed to her charm.** *Ms.* **magazine named her one of its 1986 Women of the Year, along with (from left) TV's** *Cagney & Lacey* **(Sharon Gless and Tyne Daly) and Senator Barbara Mikulski of Maryland.**

After that award, signing a new contract with CBS records three days later had to be anticlimactic for Dolly, although at the reception celebrating the contract she did get to hobnob with still more of New York's elite, including artist Andy Warhol and disco diva Grace Jones. Secure in her recovery from illness and depression, Dolly talked about them publicly for the first time a month later in an interview for *Life* magazine. She had even made peace with the hysterectomy; she's said since, "My songs are my children, and I've given life to about 3,000 of them." Later that spring she signed with

Below: **Emmylou Harris and Dolly accepting the Country Music Association "Vocal Event of the Year" award for *Trio*.** *Opposite:* **Dolly appearing on *Saturday Night Live* in 1989.**

ABC to host a one-hour variety show called, like her previous television venture, *Dolly*. The year 1987 was turning into a banner year. Dolly's triumphant return culminated with the Warner Brothers release of the *Trio* album, her long-awaited collaboration with Linda Ronstadt and Emmylou Harris.

Her ability to handle life's bumpier stretches was back as well. In the summer of 1987, midnight vandals defaced her just-unveiled bronze statue in front of the Sevier County courthouse, spray-painting it black in a mysterious protest. More seriously, the ABC show bombed and was canceled after only one season. Dolly's blithe acceptance of that failure—"It sucked," she said—and her willingness to go on to something else were ample evidence that she had regained all her resilience.

In 1989 she made her most successful film appearance since her *9 to 5* debut, playing small-town beautician Truvy Jones in the star-studded film *Steel Magnolias*. And in October of that year, she received an honor that meant more to her than most of the others: an honorary doctorate from Carson Newman College in Jefferson City, Tennessee. Formalizing her attempts to give back a little of the bounty she has received, Dolly organized the Dollywood Foundation, its primary objective to help young people in Tennessee complete their education. "Sevier County has the highest dropout rate of anywhere in the United States," she told a journalist at the time. "A lot of the kids are poor...and their parents didn't go to school [either]."

Left: **Dolly's most acclaimed performance after *9 to 5* was in *Steel Magnolias* as the warm-hearted beautician Truvy Jones; the star-studded cast included Olympia Dukakis.**
Opposite: **Dolly with Olympia Dukakis and Daryl Hannah at a cast party for *Steel Magnolias*.**

As she neared the midpoint of her fifth decade, Dolly was doing better than ever. She was dealing with approaching middle age with a typical combination of insouciance and practicality; she has made no secret of using plastic surgery to reverse any effects that might mar her carefully crafted image. "If you got those little [hip] pouches that no amount of exercise or diet's gonna get, well, you just go in for a [lipo-]sucking," she says. "If it makes you feel your best self—and as long as you don't get your surgeon from the Yellow Pages—what's wrong with it?" (And about breast surgery: "I had them little soldiers lifted at attention so I don't have to wear a bra.")

Whatever her formula was, it was working. In 1993—the same year that Whitney Houston's cover of Dolly's "I Will Always Love You" became the most popular single of all time by holding the #1 spot for a record-breaking fourteen

Previous Pages: **(left) Spoofing Madonna and (right) goofing with wrestler Terry "Hulk" Hogan.** *Above:* **For a 1993 country music festival at Radio City Music Hall, New York temporarily renamed Sixth Avenue and Fiftieth Street "Country Takes Manhattan Way" and "Dolly Parton Boulevard" respectively.** *Right:* **Dolly at a 1993 taping of *The Joan Rivers Show*.**

The Rest of the Trio:
Linda Ronstadt and Emmylou Harris

From the moment that Linda Ronstadt and Emmylou Harris sang with Dolly on her first syndicated television show, it was clear that the three should do something bigger together—though it took most of a decade before they managed to do it. They were of the same generation: the Tennessee sharecropper's daughter, the part-Mexican from Arizona, and the Alabama-born Marine Corps brat. It was not only their voices that blended; it was their histories, their personas, and their styles. If Dolly in 1987 was firmly country with a touch of pop, Ronstadt was a pop-rock belter with a touch of country, and Harris the personification of spiritualized country-rock.

Ronstadt, born in Tucson in 1946, was only six months younger than Dolly, and their careers had many parallels. In 1964, the same year Dolly rode the bus to Nashville and her struggle for stardom, Ronstadt left Tucson for Los Angeles, where she signed with Capitol Records and tried to find her niche. As Dolly was getting her first major hits in the late 1960s, Ronstadt, who was then fronting the Stone Poneys, had her first chartbuster in 1967 with "Different Drum. In 1972, she released a successful album backed by the Eagles, the superstar band of country-rock, and in 1974 had her first #1 hits with "You're No Good" and "When Will I Be Loved?"

In the late 1970s, Ronstadt hit the tabloid headlines as the "constant companion" of California's then-governor, Jerry Brown. And in the early 1980s, she broadened her musical horizons considerably, first by starring in a successful stage production of the Gilbert and Sullivan operetta *The Pirates of Penzance*, and then by releasing a series of albums in new (to her) genres, from the pop ballads of the 1930s and 1940s to the art music of composer Philip Glass. Then, in 1987, came the spectacularly well-received *Trio* album, after which Ronstadt returned to a different branch of her roots with the Spanish-language album *Canciones de mi padre (Songs of My Father)*.

Emmylou Harris, born in Birmingham, Alabama, in 1949, is the youngest of the three. The daughter of a Marine officer, she, too, had left home early to forge a career in music: Harris had come to New York City's Greenwich Village, the center of the urban folk revival, at eighteen. But folk was on its way out, and, casting about at random, Harris wound up in Washington, D.C. There she formed a short-lived but immensely fruitful partnership with the doomed singer-songwriter Gram Parsons; together, they worked out a country-rock style that received enormous acclaim when they released their 1973 album, *Grievous Angel*. But Parsons died the same year of massive alcohol abuse—he was only thirty-six years old—and Harris was left personally and artistically bereft.

She got past the tragedy, minimizing the "rock" part of her country-rock sound and moving ever closer to pure country. She had a hit single, "Sweet Dreams," on her Grammy-winning 1976 album *Elite Hotel*. In 1978 her cover of Dolly's song "To Daddy" reached the #3 spot on the country charts, and the next year she had another hit with Loretta Lynn's "Blue Kentucky Girl"; both Parton and Ronstadt sang with her on the album. By the early 1980s, her uniquely spiritual sound had put her among the most celebrated of country singers.

In addition to her recurring collaborations with Dolly and Ronstadt, Harris has by now performed with virtually every important country singer and a large proportion of rock's stars as well. Her list of singing partners includes country veteran Buck Owens, Roy Orbison, the Band, the Judds, and John Denver. One critic wrote that Harris "has been the most successful of many artists to bring country values and sounds to good songs from every genre." But perhaps, looking at the careers of the trio, their greatest success has actually been their sheer staying power. In a world that tries to discard its women stars well before they hit middle age, Ronstadt and Harris are, like Dolly, still going strong as they near—and pass—fifty.

The "Trio": Linda Ronstadt (left), Emmylou Harris (center), and Dolly.

weeks—Dolly made a successful video with the year's hottest male country star, Billy Ray Cyrus. The next year, her candid autobiography, *My Life and Other Unfinished Business*, made her a best-selling author as well. She also started her own line of cosmetics, called Beauty Confidence, and recorded still another notable collaboration: *Honky-Tonk Angels*, with country queens Loretta Lynn and Tammy Wynette.

Dolly's fiftieth birthday in 1996 found her in a very different place from the fragile state she had been in when she marked her fortieth. She was wryly amused when fans made sure no one missed the occasion by buying billboard space all around Nashville to wish her a happy birthday. "Like I really wanted that," she said to one reporter. "Now the whole world knows...."

Opposite: **The "Honky-Tonk Angels": Loretta Lynn (left), Dolly, and Tammy Wynette (right) at the Country Music Association's awards ceremony in 1993.** *Above:* **Signing her autobiography,** *My Life And Other Unfinished Business.*

But in fact she had no complaints. Now what one journalist described as an "eye-popping show-biz icon," Dolly was worth a cool one hundred million dollars in 1996, and is showing no signs of slowing down.

On the contrary, she has been taking on evermore ambitious projects. She recorded *Treasures*, a collection of country classics, with her most unlikely collaborators to date: the album included performances with John Popper of the rock band Blues Traveler; the hot young country fiddler Allison Krauss; and the South African group Ladysmith Black Mambazo. (*Treasures* was also a quiet tribute to Carl, featuring some of his favorite songs.) Dolly has planned new

business ventures, including a line of wigs. In 1996, Sandollar, the television and film production company she created with manager Sandy Gallin, had half a dozen TV specials and movies in the works. She founded a new charitable enterprise as well: The Dr. Robert F. Thomas Foundation, named for the doctor who rode through the storm to deliver her half a century before. The foundation runs the only hospital back home in Sevier County.

Few people can resist taking stock as they pass the half-century mark. In that respect, at least, Dolly is no exception. She seems very content with what she's made of herself. Of the Parton image, she says happily, "I'll be this way when I'm eighty, like Mae West. I may be on crutches [or] in a wheelchair...but I'll still have my high heels, my nails and make-up on, my hair'll be all poufed up, and my boobs'll still be hangin' out."

Of her marriage: "It is pure, it is sacred, and it is real."

Of her songwriting: "I cry, I pray, I piss and moan and cuss and write and sing my songs and [any

Above: **Dolly arrives at the 36th Annual Grammy Award Ceremonies in 1994.**
Right: **Dolly and her manager Sandy Gallin at the Los Angeles premier of *Mrs. Doubtfire*.**

Left: **Dolly kept busier than ever In the '90s, with television shows, new records, and even radio performances.** *Above:* **Dolly, the reigning queen of country, at the Country Music Association's awards ceremony in 1994.**

Dolly Parton
114

trouble] goes away. I almost feel God puts me through heartaches so I will have more to write about."

Perhaps most telling of all, though, is a simple remark she made to a journalist, one that may sum up her whole amazing odyssey in one sentence: "I still know who the little girl from Sevier is," she said. "I never lose sight of her."

Left: **Dolly celebrating her fiftieth birthday in 1996.** *Above:* **The troubles of a few years past forgotten, Dolly was triumphant at the eighth season grand opening of Dollywood.**

Selected Bibliography

Books

Clarke, Donald, ed. *The Penguin Encyclopedia of Popular Music.* London: Penguin, 1989.

Country Music Foundation. Country: *The Music and the Musicians from the Beginnings to the '90s.* New York, London, and Paris: Abbeville Press, 1994.

McCloud, Barry. *Definitive Country: The Ultimate Encyclopedia of Country Music and Its Performers.* New York: Perigee, 1995.

Parton, Dolly. *Dolly: My Life and Other Unfinished Business.* New York: HarperCollins, 1994.

Magazine and Newspaper Articles

Battle, Bob. "Threat Cancels All Dolly's Shows," *Nashville Banner,* January 19, 1983.

Chase, Chris. "The Country Girl." *The New York Times Magazine,* May 9, 1976.

"Dolly In Blackface." *Chattanooga News-Free Press,* June 19, 1987.

"Dolly Parton Talks Frankly About Her Incredible Double Life," *The Star,* May 15, 1979.

"Dolly's Show," *Houston Post,* March 24, 1987.

Flippo, Chet. "Dolly Parton." *Rolling Stone,* December, 11, 1980.

Gleason, Holly. "Dolly Parton: Here I Come Again." *Saturday Evening Post,* October, 1989.

"Good Golly, Miss Dolly." *Vogue,* January 1994.

Griffith-Roberts, Carolanne. "Hooray for Dollywood." *Southern Living,* July, 1995.

Grobel, Lawrence. "Dolly Parton." *Playboy,* October, 1978.

Grobel, Lawrence. "I Ain't Down Yet." *Redbook,* July, 1988.

Janos, Leo. "Dolly Parton: No Frets, No Regrets." *Cosmopolitan,* September, 1980.

Jerome, Jim. "One Tough Dolly." *Ladies' Home Journal,* July, 1995.

Maynard, Joyce. "What Dolly Wants Now." *McCall's,* May, 1992.

Oermann, Robert K. "Dolly Discovers 'Treasures.'" *The Tennessean*, September 28, 1996.

Parton, Willadeene. "My Sister, Dolly Parton." *McCall's*, July, 1985.

Petrucelli, Alan W. "Dolly's Spiritual Side." *Redbook*, January, 1991.

    "Talking With Dolly Parton." *Redbook*, July, 1987.

"Power and Glory from 'Ms.'" *USA Today*, January 3, 1987.

Rockwell, John. "Songs Presented By Dolly Parton." *The New York Times*, September 16, 1974.

Steinem, Gloria. "Dolly Parton." *Ms.*, January 1987.

White, Susan. Interview with Dolly Parton. *New York Daily News*, December 21, 1990.

Filmography

9 to 5, 1980

Best Little Whorehouse in Texas, 1982

Rhinestone, 1984

Steel Magnolias, 1989

Straight Talk, 1992

The Beverly Hillbillies, 1993

Selected Discography

Puppy Love (Goldband, 1960)

Hello, I'm Dolly (Monument, 1967)

Just Between You and Me—Dolly and Porter Wagoner
 (RCA, 1968)

Just Because I'm a Woman (RCA, 1968)

In the Good Old Days When Times Were Bad (RCA, 1969)

My Blue Ridge Mountain Boy (RCA, 1969)

Porter Wayne and Dolly Rebecca (RCA, 1970)

Coat of Many Colors (RCA, 1971)

My Tennessee Mountain Home (RCA, 1973)

Jolene (RCA, 1974)

Love Is Like a Butterfly (RCA, 1974)

Here You Come Again (RCA, 1977)

Dolly Parton and Kitty Wells (Exact, 1980)

9 to 5 (and Odd Jobs) (RCA, 1980)

Kris, Willie, Dolly & Brenda: The Winning Hand—Dolly,
 Kris Kristofferson,
 Willie Nelson, Brenda Lee (1982)

Once Upon a Christmas—Dolly and Kenny Rogers
 (RCA, 1984)

Trio—Dolly, Linda Ronstadt, Emmylou Harris
 (Warner Bros., 1987)

Photo Credits

Front Jacket Photography: AP / Wide World Photos

Back Jacket Photography: The Everett Collection /
©Paul Drinkwater

AP / Wide World Photos: pp. 20, 97, 104, 107

**Photographs Courtesy of the Country Music Foundation,
 Nashville:** pp. 22, 34, 35, 40, 42, 48, 49, 50, 51, 52, 55,
 56, 58, 61, 62, 74; ©Les Leverett: pp. 26, 65

Everett Collection: pp. 8, 19, 24, 45, 54, 57, 68, 77

FPG: ©Peter Borsari: pp. 12, 83; ©Travelpix: p. 38;
 ©Walter Bibikow: p. 90-91 left

©Ron Galella: pp. 79, 111; Credit: Anthony Savignano:
 pp. 2, 105; Credit: James Smeal: pp. 89, 91 right, 115

The Kobal Collection: pp. 80, 85

London Features: ©Ron Wolfson: p. 13; ©Gregg De Guire: p. 116

Michael Ochs Archives/Venice, CA: p. 47

Personality Photos: p. 92

Photofest: pp. 66, 71, 73, 84, 93, 98, 100, 117

Retna Ltd.: ©Beth Gwinn: pp. 6, 10, 108, 113;
 ©Gary Gershoff: p. 11; ©Nancy Barr: pp. 14, 16, 17,
 18, 21, 25, 28, 29, 31, 32, 36, 37, 39, 43, 44, 70, 76, 78,
 82, 87, 114; ©Redferns/A. Putler: p. 72; ©Bruno Gaget:
 p. 94; ©Steve Granitz: pp. 96, 101, 109; ©Chris Kraft:
 p. 102, 112

Reuters / Corbis-Bettmann: p. 110

Courtesy of Showtime Archives, Toronto: pp. 33, 118

UPI / Corbis Bettmann: pp. 60, 69, 75, 99, 103

Dolly Parton

118

Index